W9-CUF-965

CHARLES R. SWINDOLL

Second Wind
FOR THOSE STRUGGLING
TO GET UP AGAIN

ZondervanPublishingHouse
Grand Rapids, Michigan

A Division of HarperCollins*Publishers*

Second Wind

Copyright ®1977 by Charles R. Swindoll, Inc.

Requests for information should be addressed to: Zondervan Publishing House Grand Rapids, Michigan 49530

Library of Congress Cataloging-in-Publication Data Swindoll, Charles R. Second Wind: for those struggling to get up again / Charles R. Swindoll. p. cm. Originally published: Portland, Or.: Multnomah c1977. ISBN 0-310-42081-4 (pbk.) 1. Christian life–1960-. I. Title. [BV4501.2.S895 1994] 248.4–dc20

94-2809

CIP

Scripture quotations, unless otherwise marked, are taken from the New American Standard Bible, © The Lockman Foundation 1960, 1962, 1963, 1968, 1971, 1972, 1973, 1975, 1977, and are used by permission.

Verses marked TLB are taken from The Living Bible, © 1971 by Tyndale House Publishers, Wheaton, Ill. Used by permission.

Verses marked MLB are taken from The Modern Language Bible: The New Berkeley Version in Modern English, © 1945 by Gerrit Verkuyl, and © 1959, 1969 by Zondervan Bible Publishers, and are used by permission.

Verses marked Good News Bible are taken from the Good News Bible—Old Testament: © American Bible Society 1976: New Testament: © American Bible Society 1966, 1971, 1976. Used by permission.

Verses marked Phillips are taken from J. B. Phillips: The New Testament in Modern English, Revised Edition © J. B. Phillips 1958, 1960, 1972, and used by permission of Macmillan Publishing Co., Inc., New York; and Collins Publishers, London.

Verses marked NIV are taken from the Holy Bible: New International Version, © 1978 by the New York International Bible Society. Used by permission of Zondervan Bible Publishers.

The coed's letter is from *Failure: The Back Door to Success* by Erwin W. Lutzer, © 1976 and published by Moody Press. Used by permission.

Cover photograph ©1992 Otto Rogge/The Stock Market; *Cover design by Mark Veldheer and Gary Gnidovic*

Printed in Hong Kong

95 96 97 98 99 00/ ❖ HK /10 9 8 7 6 5 4 3 2

"O God of Second Chances and New Beginnings, Here I am again."

NANCY SPIEGELBERG

Did you ever totally blow it . . . louse up completely . . . fall flat on your face?
Are you ready to get back on your feet, grab a second wind,
and begin again?

God is a specialist at making something useful and beautiful out of
something broken and confused. He's ready to heal every hurt . . .
if you're ready to run toward tomorrow.

The Road Behind, The Road Beneath, The Road Beyond

As for us, we have this large crowd of witnesses around us. So then, let us rid ourselves of everything that gets in the way, and of the sin which holds on to us so tightly, and let us run with determination the race that lies before us.

Let us keep our eyes fixed on Jesus, on whom our faith depends from beginning to end. He did not give up because of the cross! On the contrary, because of the joy that was waiting for him, he thought nothing of the disgrace of dying on the cross, and he is now seated at the right side of God's throne.

Think of what he went through; how he put up with so much hatred from sinners! So do not let yourselves become discouraged and give up.

(HEBREWS 12:1–3, GOOD NEWS BIBLE)

The Road Behind

*"God wants to use you—
stumbling and all—but He won't do so
if you refuse to get up."*

Photograph by Mark Veldheer

Starting where you are

To start over you have to know where you are. To get somewhere else it's necessary to know where you're presently standing. That's true in a department store or a big church, on a freeway or a college campus—or in *life,* for that matter. Very, very seldom does anybody "just happen" to end up on the right road. The process involved in redirecting our lives is often painful, slow, and even confusing. Occasionally it seems unbearable.

Take Jonah. (No one else wanted to.) He was prejudiced, bigoted, stubborn, openly rebellious, and spiritually insensitive. Other prophets ran *to* the Lord. He ran *from* Him. Others declared the promises of God with fervent zeal. Not Jonah. He was about as motivated as a six-hundred-pound grizzly in mid-January.

Somewhere down the line the prophet got his inner directions cross-wired. He wound up, of all places, on a ship in the Mediterranean Sea bound for a place named Tarshish. That was due west. God had told him *Nineveh*. That was due east. (That's like flying from Los Angeles to Berlin by way of Honolulu.) But Jonah never got to Tarshish, as you may remember. Through a traumatic chain of events, Jonah began to get his head together in the digestive tract of a gigantic fish.

What a place to start over! Slopping around in the seaweed and juices inside that monster, fishing for a match to find his way out, Jonah took a long, honest look at his short, dishonest life. For the first time in a long time, the prophet brushed up on his prayer life. He yelled for mercy. He recited psalms. He promised the Lord that he would keep his vow and get back on target. Only one creature on earth felt sicker than Jonah—the fish, in whose belly Jonah bellowed. Up came the prophet, who hit the road running—*toward Nineveh.*

One of the most encouraging things about new years, new weeks, and new days is the word *new.* Webster reveals its meaning: "refreshed, different from one of the same that has existed previously . . . unfamiliar." Best of all, it's a place to start over. Refresh yourself. Change directions. Begin anew.

But that requires knowing where you are. It requires taking time to honestly admit your present condition. It means facing the music, standing alone inside the fish and coming to terms with those things that need attention, fishing in the seaweed for a match. *Before you find your way out, you must determine where you are.* Exactly. Once that is accomplished, you're ready to start over.

Just as there are few atheists in foxholes, so there are few rebels in fish stomachs. Perhaps you can identify rather easily with Jonah. This hasn't been your all-time-spiritual-high-plateau year, right? You've dodged and ducked, squirmed and squeaked your way through one Tarshish trip after another. But no more. You're tired. *Exhausted* says it better. Swallowed alive by your circumstances says it best. You feel oppressed, guilty, overused, and underdeveloped. You're not that old . . . but you've run a long way. Few moons but many miles. A subtle whisper in your ear says, "You're through. Finished. Burned out. Used up. You've been replaced . . . forgotten."

That's a lie! A carefully-timed deception by the enemy of your soul. Look at what the prophet Joel writes to all the Jonahs who may be reading this book. God is speaking:

> *I will make up to you for the years that the swarming locust has eaten . . .* (Joel 2:25a).

If God can take a disobedient prophet, turn him around and set him on fire spiritually, He can do the same with *you*. He is a Specialist at making something useful and beautiful out of something broken and confused.

Where are you? Start *there*. Openly and freely declare your need to the One who cares deeply. Don't hide a thing. Show God all those locust bites. He's ready to heal every one—if you're ready to run toward that Nineveh called tomorrow.

THE BROKEN WING

It is quite probable that someone reading my words this moment is fighting an inner battle with a ghost from the past. The skeleton in one of yesterday's closets is beginning to rattle louder and louder. Putting adhesive tape around the closet and moving the bureau in front of the door does little to muffle the clattering bones. You wonder, possibly, "Who knows?" You think, probably, "I've had it . . . can't win . . . party's over."

The anchor that tumbled off your boat is dragging and snagging on the bottom. Guilt and anxiety have come aboard, pointing out the great dark hulks of shipwrecks below. They busy themselves drilling worry-holes in your hull and you are beginning to sink. Down in the hold you can hear them chant an old lie as they work: "The bird with the broken pinion never soared as high again. . . ."

Allow me to present a case in opposition to these destructive and inaccurate accusers. It may be true that you've done or experienced things which would embarrass you if they became public knowledge. You may have committed a terrible and tragic sin that was never traced back to you. You may have a criminal record or a moral charge or a domestic conflict that, to this moment, is private information. You may wrestle with a past that has been fractured and wounded by a mental or emotional breakdown. Futile attempts at suicide may add to the previous scar tissue and increase your fear of being labeled "sick" or "nervous." It is possible that you live with memories, covered now by the sands of time, of an illicit relationship or a financial failure or a terrible habit or a divorce or a scandalous involvement. You feel that any one of these things might mar or cripple your reputation if the dirty details ever spilled on the table of gluttonous gossipers.

But wait a minute. Before you surrender your case as hopeless, consider the liberating evidence offered in the Bible. Take an honest look at men and women whom God used *in spite of* their past! *Abraham,* founder of Israel and tagged "the friend of God," was once a worshiper of idols. *Joseph* had a prison record but later became prime minister of Egypt. *Moses* was a murderer, but later became the one who delivered his nation from the slavery of Pharaoh. *Jephthah* was an illegitimate child who ran around with a tough bunch of hoods before he was chosen by God to become His personal representative. *Rahab* was a harlot in the streets of Jericho but was later used in such a mighty way that God listed her among the members of His hall of fame in Hebrews 11.

Still unconvinced? There's more. *Eli* and *Samuel* were both poor, inconsistent fathers, but proved to be strong men in God's hand regardless. *Jonah* and *John Mark* were missionaries who ran away from hardship like cowards but were ever so profitable later on. *Peter* openly denied the Lord and cursed Him, only to return and become God's choicest spokesman among the early years of the infant church. *Paul* was so hard and vicious in his early life the disciples and apostles refused to believe he'd actually become a Christian—but you know how greatly God used him. We could go on and on. The files of heaven are filled with stories of redeemed, refitted renegades and rebels.

How magnificent is grace! How malignant is guilt! How sweet are the promises! How sour is the past! How precious and broad is God's love! How petty and narrow are man's limitations! How refreshing is the Lord! How rigid is the legalist!

There is not a single saint who sits in a single church free from a few things he or she is ashamed of—not one of us! The one who thinks otherwise is worse than all the rest combined. In plain, garden variety English, we were all taken from the same dunghill. And so we all fight the same fight with the filth of the flesh regardless of how loudly we sing, how piously we pray, or how sweetly we say hello.

Mark it—when God forgives, He forgets. He is not only willing but pleased to use any vessel—just as long as it is clean *today*. It may be cracked or chipped. It may be worn or it may have never been used before. You can count on this—the past ended one second ago. From this point onward, you can be clean, filled with His Spirit, and used in many different ways for His honor. God's glorious grace says: "Throw guilt and anxiety overboard . . . draw the anchor . . . trim the sails . . . man the rudder . . . a strong gale is coming!"

IN THE SHADE
OF A JUNIPER

A *major portion* of our eye troubles could probably be diagnosed "ingrownius eyeballitus." Ingrown eyeballs. It strikes us all. In both dramatic and subtle ways, the stubborn enemy of our souls urges us to look ever inward instead of outward and upward. He whispers little nothings in our ears. He reminds us of how unappreciated and ill-treated we are . . . how important yet overlooked . . . how gifted yet ignored . . . how capable yet unrecognized . . . how bright yet eclipsed . . . how valuable yet unrewarded.

This clever adversary slips into the office of the faithful worker who has been bypassed, unpromoted. Looking up from his cluttered desk, the worker's mind is suddenly swamped with the silt of self-pity. Slipping down the hall and into the sickroom of the sufferer; the enemy pauses long enough to announce: "You've been forgotten. No one cares about you—not really. Out of sight, out of mind." Kneeling behind the bench warmer he whispers, "Face it, man, first string is out of reach. You'll never make it." To the unemployed he says, "No chance!" To the divorced he says, "No place!" To the bereaved he says, "No hope!" To the struggling he says, "No way."

The most damaging impact of self-pity is its ultimate end. Cuddle and nurse it as an infant and you'll have on your hands in a brief period of time a beast, a monster, a raging, coarse brute that will spread the poison of bitterness and paranoia throughout your system. A frown will soon replace your smile. A pungent criticism will replace a pleasant, "I understand." Suspicion and resentment will submerge your selfish island like a tidal wave. You will soon discover that the sea of self-pity has brought with it prickly urchins of doubt, despair, and even the desire to die.

An exaggeration? A wild imagination? If you think so, sit with me beneath the shade of a juniper tree located at 19 First Kings, the address of a prophet named Elijah. The leather-girded prophet had just finished mopping up a victory over Ahab and his Baal-worshiping cronies. God stamped His approval upon Elijah in such a way that all Israel realized he was God's mouthpiece. At this point Jezebel, Ahab's spouse (he was her mouse), declared and predicted Elijah's death within twenty-four hours. Surely the seasoned prophet had faced criticism before. He lived with bad press and constant threats—all prophets do. That's par for the course! But this threat somehow found its mark in a chink of his armor.

Elijah ran for his life. Finally, ninety miles later, he collapsed beneath a juniper tree. Overwhelmed with self-pity, the prophet whined, "I've had enough—take away my life. I've got to die sometime, and it might as well be now."

Later on he admitted:

I have worked very hard for the Lord God of the heavens; but the people of Israel have broken their covenant with you and torn down your altars and killed your prophets, and only I am left; and now they are trying to kill me, too (1 Kings 19:10, TLB).

There you have it. Self-pity in the raw. Elijah's eyes were so ingrown he saw two of everything—except God. He felt unloved, cast off, and out of it. Most of all he believed his situation so isolated him that he, only, was left. Nobody else was near and in the prophet's mind that included God. Self-pity is the smog that pollutes and obscures the light of the Son. The more you're out in it, the deeper it hurts. The more your eyes shed tears, the greater the sting of loneliness.

But God didn't rebuke His man. He didn't club him nor did He strike him dead. Instead, He encouraged him to take a long rest and enjoy a catered meal or two. Jehovah helped Elijah get his eyes off himself and his situation. Gently, He prodded the prophet to focus anew on his God. A little later the Lord gave him a close friend named Elisha with whom he might share his life and his load.

Feeling sorry for yourself today? Caught in that ancient "sin-drome" of self-pity? Why not try God's remedy: A good, well-deserved mental rest where you stop trying to work things out *yourself* . . . a decent, well-balanced diet . . . a long, well-needed look at your Savior in His Word . . . topped off with some quality time with a friend.

You will be amazed at the outcome. You may even discover that what you thought was approaching blindness was only an advanced case of ingrown eyeballs.

THE GHOST
OF EPHRAIM

❧

P*salm 78 is* a hymn of history. Being a
Maskil psalm, it is designed to instruct those who pon-
der its message. The opening words command us to
"listen" . . . "to incline our ears" to what the composer, Asaph, has to
say. Immediately we realize that he is recounting the unhappy days of
disobedience which characterized the Jews during their rebellion and
wandering. Throughout the psalm Asaph contrasts God's faithfulness
and patience with Israel's failure and unbelief. The ancient hymn was, no

Photograph ©1994 Michael Hudson

doubt, sung in a minor key.

My eye fell upon verse 9 recently as I was on a safari through the Scriptures. I was intrigued by a strange stroke of the psalmist's pen:

The sons of Ephraim were archers equipped with bows, yet they turned back in the day of battle (Psalm 78:9).

These men of Ephraim were adept with bow and arrow. Furthermore, they had sufficient hardware to handle the enemy's attack. They possessed both skill and supplies in abundance . . . but you couldn't tell it! On the "day of battle" (that is, the first day of the fray) they "turned back." Like foxes hunted by hounds, they ran. The sound of battle made them as nervous as a long-tailed cat in a room full of rocking chairs. Although well-armed and capable with their weapons, they lacked steadfastness. On the surface they were a highly-polished, impressive-looking, rugged company of muscular men. They were as smooth as a Marine drill team, running through the manual of arms like a fine-tuned machine. No one faulted E Company at inspection. Everyone's sandals shone like polished chrome. But underneath the dressblues, written across their soft underbelly, was a more accurate description—*coward*. The fastest maneuver they ever accomplished was the waving of a white flag. The only weapon they ever used to restrain the enemy was a cloud of dust as they retreated en masse, in a hurry.

What an indictment! The sons of Ephraim loved Memorial Day parades and target practice, but as soon as the going got tough, they ran right out of their shiny sandals, heading back to the barracks. The original *quitters*. Discipline and guts were nasty words in the Ephraim camp. Their watchword was EASE and their slogan was MAKE A GOOD APPEARANCE. But behind the thin veneer of valor was the brittle, plastic shell of surrender.

Ephraimites live on, you know. They have invaded the ranks of churches and families and until difficulty comes, you cannot spot them. They ape the lifestyle of heroic saints to perfection. Their words and prayers, verses and vows shine like Ephraim's arrows at dawn. But let the hot rays of hardship beat upon their backs and they melt like butter on the back burner. They just can't handle the battle . . . they can't take the pressure . . . they opt for the easy way out. They run. They come for counsel but reject the demands of Scripture. They want a medicine man with a quick cure, not direct advice to repent, reestablish biblical relationships, and restore God's method for living.

On a Los Angeles radio talk show, author Anna Sklar uncovered an incredible statistic from her book, *Runaway Wives*. Ten years ago for every wife or mother who walked away from her home and responsibilities . . . 600 husbands and fathers did so. Today, for each man who now does that, two women do.

Selah! Pause and let that sink in.

Understand, I'm not advocating either, nor taking sides that one is better than another. I am simply amazed at the unbelievably rapid rise in modern-day women who choose escape as a favorite method of "coping." Contrary to our great American heritage, many of today's citizens would rather switch than fight . . . or, quite honestly, quit than stick. That which was once not even an option is now standard operating procedure—the preferred plan to follow. Homes and churches across the country are haunted by ghosts of the Ephraimites.

The quitting habit creates a strange undertow which complicates rather than corrects our difficulties. The ability to "turn off" responsibilities is now in vogue. Much of the literature of our day that promotes this Ephraimitish reaction draws its ideas from the mid-sixties where "dropping out" was first peddled by Timothy Leary and his drugged disciples. There was a time when the going got tough, the tough got going. No longer! Now it's, if you start to sink, *jump,* don't bail. It's, if it gets hard, *quit,* don't bother.

"Let's just quit" are household words. A marriage gets shaky and hits a few hard jolts—"Let's just quit." School is expensive, tedious, and demanding—"Let's just quit." A job increases in responsibility, you get flack from the boss or the public, no one appreciates you—"Let's just quit." When a personal dream or goal in life is met with hurdles and hardship—both goal and dream are soon forgotten. Before long we begin to resemble Rome in its last days—a magnificent mask of outward, impressive stature . . . devoid of inner strength . . . soft and mushy at the core, desperately lacking in discipline and determination.

There is not an achievement worth remembering that isn't stained with the blood of diligence and etched with the scars of disappointment. To run, to quit, to escape, even *to hide,* solves nothing . . . it only postpones a reckoning with reality. It may feel good now, but it's disaster when the bills come due.

Are you facing some difficult battle today? Don't run! Stand still . . . and refuse to retreat. Look at it as God looks at it and draw upon His power to hold up under the blast. Sure, it's tough. Nobody ever said the Christian life was easy. God never promised you a Disneyland. He offers something better—His own sustaining presence through any trouble we may encounter.

I've never been much of an admirer of Harry S. Truman—but I did, at times, appreciate his grit. The battle often raged during his presidency and on one occasion he responded to it with the words:

If you don't like the heat, get out of the kitchen!

I've not met anyone who was able to stay strong without some time in the kitchen. Ephraimites are terribly undernourished. So my advice is a little different from Truman's:

If you don't like the heat— stay in the kitchen and learn to handle it!

A MESSAGE
FOR MISFITS

❧

Before he ever came to the plate, Jephthah had three strikes against him.

- He was an illegitimate child. *Strike one.*
- He was the son of a barmaid and a brute. *Strike two.*
- He was raised in an atmosphere of hatred and hostility. *Strike three.*

Nurtured in an overcrowded cage of half-brothers, he was the constant target of verbal put-downs and violent profanity. Putting it mildly,

Jephthah wasn't wanted. He compensated by becoming the meanest kid on the block.

Kicked out of home before he reached young manhood, he took up the lifestyle of a rebel among a tough bunch of thugs that hobnobbed in a place called Tob. Earning a reputation as the hardest hardguy, he was elected leader of a gang. They ripped and rammed their way through villages like a pack of wild hyenas. Had they ridden motorcycles, their black leather jackets could have read "The Tob Mob" as they raced over the hills, outrunning the law of the land. Read Judges 11:1–3 for yourself. It's all there. A societal reject, Jephthah was Charles Manson, the Boston Strangler, and Clyde Barrow all wrapped up in one explosive body. Having him and his apes drop into the Tob Pharmacy for Saturday night malts was about as comfortable as taking a swim with the Loch Ness monster.

Suddenly, a change occurred. The people of Israel encountered a barrage of hostilities from their not-so-friendly neighbors to the east—the

Ammonites. The longer the battle raged against this hateful enemy tribe, the more obvious it became that Israel was against the ropes. Defeat was inevitable. The Jews needed a leader with guts to stand up against the fiery foes from Ammon. Guess who the Israelites thought of. Right! They figured that only a guy with his record would qualify for the job, so they called the man from Tob. Tremblingly, they said:

Come and be our chief that we may fight against the sons of Ammon . . . and [you may] become head over all the inhabitants of Gilead (Judges 11:6,8).

What a deal! Asking Jephthah if he could fight was like asking Al Hirt if he could blow some jazz or A. J. Foyt if he could drive you around the block. That was Jephthah's day in court. After a brief cat-and-mouse interchange, the mobster signed the dotted line. Predictably, he annihilated the Ammonites in short order and the Tob Evening News rolled off the presses with the headline:

HOODLUM BECOMES HERO—EX-CON ELECTED JUDGE!

Jephthah the judge. Fellow gangsters had to call him "Your Honor." What a switch! He fit the throne about as appropriately as Fidel Castro would fit in the White House. Jephthah had no rightful claim to such a high calling.

That would have been true—except for one thing: GOD's GRACE. Remember now, God is the One who builds trophies from the scrap pile . . . who draws His clay from under the bridge . . . who makes clean instruments of beauty from the filthy failures of yesteryear.

To underscore this truth, consider Paul's stunning remark made to a group of unsophisticated Corinthian Christians:

> *Do not be deceived: Neither the sexually immoral nor idolaters nor adulterers nor male prostitutes nor homosexual offenders nor thieves nor the greedy nor drunkards nor slanderers nor swindlers will inherit the kingdom of God. And that is what some of you were* (1 Corinthians 6:9–11a, NIV).

Don't rush over those last eight words:

And that is what some of you were. . . .

Our Father, in great grace, loved *us* when you and I were Jephthah—a rebel or a drunk or a gossip or a crook or a liar or a brawler or a Pharisee or a playboy or an adulteress or a hypocrite or a do-gooder or a drop-out or a drug addict. Looking for sinners, He found us in desperate straits. Lifting us to the level of His much-loved Son, He brought us in, washed our wounds, and changed our direction. All our church-going and hymn-singing and long-praying and committee-sitting and religious-talking will never ease the fact that we were dug from a deep, dark, deathly pit. And may we *never* forget it. Classic misfits . . . we.

But there is one major difference between Jephthah and us. God chose to *reveal* his past for everyone to read. But He chose to hide ours so none would ever know what colossal misfits we really are.

Talk about grace!

FOR THOSE
WHO STUMBLE

~

Snake River Canyon coiled up,
rattled its tail, and sank its fangs into its would-be cap-
tor. On a sultry Sunday afternoon its 1,700-foot jaws
yawned wide as it swallowed a strange-tasting capsule prescribed for it
by Dr. Robert C. Truax, the scientist-designer of *Sky Cycle X-2*. Starring
in the show was a guy some people tagged Captain Marvel, who looked
more like Billy Batson unable to remember the magic word. But before
we label him a showman . . . or a show-off . . . I suggest we consider the

outcome of this showdown.

Any third grader could have told you the vaunted skycycle leap across the canyon was a triple-A flop—a classic fizzle. The sky cycle gave up in mid-air; the driver floated to safety beneath a nylon cloud. But you won't find him sitting long-faced in a dark corner today. Most people send an ambulance and a wrecker to mop up their mistakes. He could have sent a Brink's armored car. As bystanders shouted, "Rip off!" he was thinking about write-offs. Anyone who can walk away from a failure with a smile, a bulging rear pocket, and his pride still intact has to have *something* going for him. The real six-million-dollar man, if you can believe it, is a two-wheeled wonder named Evel Knievel. Nobody—but *nobody,* in the long history of sports, ever came off a more abysmal failure better than he. The remains of Dr. Truax's flopcycle littered the canyon, but the man who took off like a bird made out like a banker.

When you stop and think it over, there's an abiding truth in that Idaho extravaganza all of us ought to capture and cultivate. It's much greater than money and far deeper than a canyon jump. There's a philosophy of life here I'm now convinced is worth one's pursuit. Here it is:

THE PERSON WHO SUCCEEDS IS NOT THE ONE WHO HOLDS BACK, FEARING FAILURE, NOR THE ONE WHO NEVER FAILS . . . BUT RATHER THE ONE WHO MOVES ON IN SPITE OF FAILURE.

As Lowell wrote:

Not failure, but low aim, is crime.

As Teddy Roosevelt believed:

Far better it is to dare mighty things, to win glorious triumphs, even though checkered by failure, than to take rank with those poor spirits who neither enjoy much nor suffer much because they live in the gray twilight that knows neither victory nor defeat.

Give me a sky cycle and a 180 foot take-off ramp with all its risks any day—before you sentence me to the path of predictability between the stone walls of routine and fear. God asks that we believe Him *regardless* of the risks—in spite of the danger—ignoring the odds. The ancient city of Jericho was defeated because Joshua and his troops defied the "normal procedure" of battle . . . never once fearing failure. The Gentiles heard of Christ Jesus because Paul and a few companions kept getting back up after being knocked down. Peter's two letters are in the Book because he refused to live in the shadow of his bad track record.

Great accomplishments are often attempted but only occasionally reached. What is interesting (and encouraging) is that those who reach them are usually those who missed many times before. Failures, you see, are only temporary tests to prepare us for permanent triumphs.

Whoever you are today—listen to me! Sitting there licking your wounds will only result in a bitter aftertaste. Sighs and tears and thoughts of quitting are understandable for the moment but *inexcusable* for the future. Get up and get on with it! Nothing damages our dignity like stumbling. Nothing destroys our life like lying there in the mud—refusing to stand up and shake it off.

Evel Knievel isn't the only one who takes spectacular tumbles. I have seen people, dressed to the hilt, stumble and fall flat on their faces as they were walking to church. I have witnessed serious and gifted soloists, stepping up to the pulpit with music in hand, stumble and fall as the sheets of music sailed like maple leaves in an October breeze. I've watched a sure and winning touchdown by a fleet split end—nobody within fifteen yards—foiled by a stumble. I've looked on as brides and grooms stumbled in unison . . . as bandsmen stumbled in formation . . . as shoppers stumbled in stores . . . as rigid Marine officers stumbled while inspecting the troops . . . as elite, elegant ladies stumbled on stage . . . as emcees got tangled in mike wires and stumbled off stage . . . as cap and gown grads stumbled to their knees receiving diplomas . . . and as an experienced, well-respected, eloquent speaker stumbled and fell just before he began to speak. I could never forget that one because in the fall he cut his lip and delivered his entire address while wiping the blood off his face!

Can you remember when you have stumbled? Nothing is more humiliating or embarrassing than spilling our dignity as we fall flat on our pride. The first thing we do is take a quick look around to see who might have noticed. We long to become *invisible*. Some of my stumbling experiences make me shudder just to call them to mind.

But do you know something? Almost without exception the response of onlookers is sympathy . . . identification with the embarrassment . . . mutual ache . . . a deep sense of inner support. In fact, the immediate response is to help the stumbler back to his feet. I cannot remember a single occasion when anyone who stumbled was held down or stepped on by those nearby. I recall that there was instant concern for their hurt feelings and their physical welfare. I also recall that everyone who tripped got right back on his feet, shrugged off the momentary humiliation, and forged ahead. There's something to be learned, my friend, in all this business of stumbling.

In the penetrating letter of James, every verse is like a scalpel—cutting deep incisions in our conscience. Hidden within James 3:2 is something we often forget:

For we all stumble in many ways.

What's he saying? To stumble is normal . . . a fact of life . . . an act that guarantees our humanness. Perhaps you have just stumbled as you read this today. Your sky cycle stalled half way up the ramp. You opened your mouth and devastated someone with a bitter remark. You feel guilty, you feel like a failure. You wish like crazy you hadn't done what you did . . . or responded like that. You're miserable, discouraged, and you'd like to hide or—better still—crawl off and die. Ridiculous! Climb out of that canyon, brush off the dirt with the promise of God's forgiveness—and move on!

Now I must add a word of realism. Instead of receiving the normal reaction of concern and support, you may find that some who saw you fall will want to hold you down or bad-mouth you because you slipped. Ignore them completely! They have forgotten that James 3:2 includes *them*. The only difference is that you didn't get to see them stumble. But they have, believe me, they have.

Not all of us plunge a sky cycle into a canyon in front of TV cameras or trip over a microphone cord before a thousand watching eyes. But we *all* stumble in many ways. What all of this adds up to is not difficult to discover.

GOD WANTS TO USE YOU—STUMBLING AND ALL—BUT HE WON'T DO SO IF YOU REFUSE TO GET UP.

Stumblers who *give up* are a dime a dozen. In fact, they're useless. Stumblers who *get up* are as rare as rubies. In fact, they're priceless.

The Road Beneath

*"If finding God's way in the suddenness of storms
makes our faith grow broad,
then trusting God's wisdom in the dailyness of living
makes it grow deep."*

A WAY IN THE STORM

Blow *that layer* of dust off the book of Nahum in your Bible and catch a glimpse of the last part of verse three, Chapter 1:

> *The way of the LORD is in the whirlwind and in the storm . . .*
> (MLB).

That's good to remember when you're in a rip-snortin', Texas frog-strangler as I was a few years back. I nudged myself to remember God's presence as the rain-heavy, charcoal clouds hemorrhaged in eerie, aerial explosions of saw-toothed lightning and reverberating thunder. Witnessing that atmospheric drama, I reminded myself of its Director who was, once again, having His way in the whirlwind and the storm. Nahum and I took the Texas highway through Weatherford, Cisco, Abilene, and Sweetwater. There was no doubt but that the Lord, the God of the heavens, was in the storm. Nature refuses to let you forget her Artist.

But life too has its storms. Hurricanes that descend from blue, sun-drenched skies or clear, starry nights. What about the whirlwinds of disease, disaster, and death? What about the storms of interruptions, irritations, and ill treatment? If Nahum's words apply to the heavenly sphere, do they also apply to the earthly? Surely if God's way is in the murky, threatening sky, it is also in the difficult, heart-straining contingencies of daily living. The Director of the heavenly and earthly theaters is One . . . and the same. The cast may be different, the plot may be altered, the props may be rearranged, but just offstage stands the Head, the Chief . . . overseeing every act, every scene, every line.

Ask Nebuchadnezzar. He would reply:

*And all the inhabitants of the earth are accounted as nothing,
but He does according to His will in the host of heaven and among
the inhabitants of earth; and no one can ward off His hand or say
to Him, "What hast Thou done?"* (Daniel 4:35).

David, if asked, would answer:

But our God is in the heavens; He does whatever He pleases
(Psalm 115:3).

Paul would add:

*For it is God who is at work in you, both to will and to work
for His good pleasure* (Philippians 2:13).

Moses nailed it down with his comment:

When you are in distress and all these things have come upon you . . . you will return to the LORD *your* God and listen to His voice (Deuteronomy 4:30).

Life is literally filled with God-appointed storms. It would take several volumes much bulkier than this one to list the whirlwinds in the walk of a Christian. But two things should comfort us in the midst of daily lightning and thunder and rain and wind. First, these squalls surge across *everyone's* horizon. God has no favorite actors who always get the leading role. Second, we all *need* them. God has no other method more effective. The massive blows and shattering blasts (not to mention the little, constant irritations) smooth us, humble us, and compel us to submit to *His* script and *His* chosen role for our lives.

William Cowper could take the stand in defense of all I have written. During one period of his life heavy, persistent clouds choked out all sunlight and hope. He tried to end it all one bleak morning by swallowing poison. The attempt at suicide failed. He then hired a coach, was driven to the Thames River, intending to hurl himself over the bridge . . . but was "strangely restrained." The next morning he fell on a sharp knife—and broke the blade! Failing in this method, he tried to hang himself but was found and taken down unconscious . . . still alive. Some time later he picked up a Bible and began to read the book of Romans. It was there Cowper finally met the God of storms, submitting to the One who had pursued him through so many desolate days and windy nights. In the center of the storm, he found peace.

After a rich life of Christian experiences—but not without whirlwind and storm—Cowper sat down and recorded his summary of the Lord's dealings with familiar words:

God moves in a mysterious way
His wonders to perform;
He plants His footsteps in the sea,
And rides upon the storm.

Deep in unfathomable mines
Of never-failing skill
He treasures up His bright designs,
And works His sovereign will.

Before the dust settles, why not ask God to have His way in today's whirlwind? The play is so much more enjoyable when the cast cooperates with the Director.

LONG WINDS,
DEEP ROOTS

Mrs. Moses' cookbook surely
had a special section on "A-Thousand-and-One Ways to
Fix Manna." Unless I miss my guess, she had tried them
all . . . *ninety-nine times*. What potatoes are to Idaho, pineapples to
Hawaii, wheat to Kansas, and crab gumbo to New Orleans, manna was
to the wandering Hebrews for forty weary years (Exodus 16:35). They
boiled it, baked it, broiled it, barbecued it, breaded it, and buttered it.

They ate it cold, hot, raw, cooked, sliced for sandwiches, baked in pies, and sprinkled on their cereal. You name it—they tried it.

When everyone came in to eat, they didn't ask, "What's for supper?" but, "How'd you fix it?" Mealtime was about as exciting as watching paint dry or listening to the minutes of last year's meeting. The most familiar sound around the table was not slurping or smacking. It was *gagging*. Oh, how they hated it. Numbers 11 tells us they actually lost their appetite because they were sick of all that manna. Everyone remembered the fish, cucumbers, leeks, onions, garlic, and melons back in Egypt—and you've got to be pretty miserable to dream of a combination plate like that.

Hold on here! Let's fine-tune that picture. A closer look at the circumstances paints a different scene altogether. Let me explain. These people didn't have to work for their food or clothing . . . not one day for forty years! Every morning, instead of going out to get the newspaper like you and I do, they gathered up the day's groceries—delivered to their front door. For forty years! There was no inflation, no sales tax, and no long lines at the checkout counter. Just a constant, daily supply of nourishing food. As a matter of fact, God called it *food from heaven . . . the bread of angels* (Psalm 78:24–25).

Accompanying this morning miracle was the faithful cloud by day and the comforting fire by night which gave them visible assurance of God's presence and protection. When thirst came, He quenched it with water that flowed from rocks like rivers. Those people enjoyed a perpetual catering service without cost, limit, labor, or hassle. All they had to do was show up, look up, eat up, and clean up.

Yet for all of this, they came to the place where they resented heavenly-cooked angels' bread. Already having much they now wanted more. Having plenty, they now wanted variety. Having tired of manna, they now wanted meat.

Exodus 16:4 provides additional insight often overlooked:

> *. . . the LORD said to Moses, "Behold, I will rain bread from*

heaven . . . and the people shall go out and gather a day's portion
every day, that I may test them. . . ."

Look carefully at the last five words. The manna was more than it appeared to be—basically, it was a *test*. It was God's examination, carefully planned, wisely implemented, and administered on a daily basis (note in the verse especially the phrase *every day*). God custom-designed the diet to be a day after day, week after week test of their obedience, their patience, and their determination to persevere in spite of the monotony of the manna. The exam results came back with a big red F across the front.

When I was only a boy, the Swindolls occasionally enjoyed a family reunion at my grandfather's bay cottage near the gulf in deep South Texas. Since the crowds were so large, we'd hire the same man each time to help with the cooking. His name was Coats. His skin was as black as a cast-iron skillet and his quick smile and quaint comments are a lasting memory to me. I remember standing near Coats one evening at sunset, watching him smear the sauce on the chunks of beef cooking slowly over a pit of coals. He was telling me about his life, which had been etched with trouble and tragedy. He rubbed his big, leathery hand through my white hair as he knelt down to my height and said:

Little Charles—the hardest thing about life is that it's so daily.

A simple way to say it, but what could be more true? *Life is so daily.* The tests that come like a flash and last no longer than a dash seldom do more than bring a brief crash. But the marathons—the relentless, incessant, persistent, continual tests that won't go away—ah, these are the ones that bruise but build character. Since virtue is not hereditary, God dispenses His test of manna to each saint in each generation, watching to see if there will be a heavenly appetite to accept a heavenly food.

If finding God's way in the suddenness of storms makes our faith grow broad, then trusting God's wisdom in the "dailyness" of living makes it grow deep. And strong.

Whatever may be your circumstances—however long it may have lasted—wherever you may be today, I bring this reminder: The stronger the winds, the deeper the roots, and the longer the winds . . . the more beautiful the tree.

THE STING
OF PEARLS

G ot your yellow pad and nickel pencil out? If not, just stop long enough to make a mental list of some of the things that irritate you. Here are a few suggestions that will get you started:

traffic jams	cold food	squeaking doors
talkative people	interruptions	incompetence
long lines	reminders	flat tires
crying babies	deadlines	balancing checkbooks

phone calls	nosy neighbors	doing dishes
misplaced keys	being rushed	mothers-in-law
untrained pets	late planes	weeds
stuck zippers	tight clothes	high prices
	peeling onions	

Any of those make you want to grind your teeth? Some of it sounds like today, doesn't it? It's easy to get the feeling that you can't win—no matter how hard you try. You start to entertain the thought I saw printed rather hurriedly on a small wooden plaque several weeks ago:

I am planning to have a nervous breakdown. I have earned it . . . I deserve it . . . I have worked hard for it . . . and nobody's going to keep me from having it!

If it weren't for irritations we'd be very patient, wouldn't we? We could wade calmly through life's placid sea and never encounter a ripple. Unfortunately, irritations comprise the major occupational hazard of the human race. One of these days it should dawn upon our minds that we'll never be completely free from irritations as long as we tread Planet Earth. Never. Upon arriving at such a profound conclusion, it would be wise to consider an alternative to losing our cool. The secret is *adjusting*.

Sure, that sounds simple. But it isn't. Several things tend to keep us on the ulcerated edge of irritability. If we lived in the zoo, the sign outside our cage might read: Human Being—Creature of Habit. We tend to develop habit reactions, wrong though they may be. We are also usually in a hurry . . . inordinately wedded to the watch on our wrist. Furthermore, many of our expectations for the day are unrealistic. Echoing in our heads are the demanding voices of objectives that belong to a *week*, rather than a single day. All of this makes the needle on our inner pressure gauge whirl like Mario Andretti's tachometer. When you increase the heat to our highly pressurized system by a fiery irritation or two . . . or three . . . BOOM! Off goes the lid and out comes the steam.

It helps me if I remember that God is in charge of my day . . . not I.

While He is pleased with the wise management of time and intelligent planning from day to day, He is mainly concerned with the development of inner character. He charts growth toward maturity, concerning Himself with the cultivation of priceless, attractive qualities that make us Christlike down deep within. One of His preferred methods of training us is through adjustment to irritation.

A perfect illustration? The oyster and its pearl.

Pearls are the product of pain. For some unknown reason, the shell of the oyster gets pierced and an alien substance—a grain of sand—slips inside. On the entry of that foreign irritant, all the resources within the tiny, sensitive oyster rush to the spot and begin to release healing fluids that otherwise would have remained dormant. By and by the irritant is covered and the wound is healed—by *a pearl*. No other gem has so fascinating a history. It is the symbol of stress—a healed wound . . . a precious, tiny jewel conceived through irritation, born of adversity, nursed by adjustments. Had there been no wounding, no irritating interruption, there could have been no pearl. Some oysters are never wounded . . . and those who seek for gems toss them aside, fit only for stew.

No wonder our heavenly home has as its entrance *pearly* gates! Those who go through them need no explanation. They are the ones who have been wounded, bruised, and have responded to the sting of irritations with the pearl of adjustment.

J. B. Phillips must have realized this as he paraphrased James 1:2–4:

> *When all kinds of trials crowd into your lives, my brothers, don't resent them as intruders, but welcome them as friends! Realize that they have come to test your endurance. But let the process go on until that endurance is fully developed, and you will find you have become men [and women] of mature character.*

THE CRY
FROM A CAVE

The Cave of Adullam was no Holiday Inn. It was a wicked refugee camp . . . a dark vault on the side of a cliff that reached deeply into a hill. Huddled in this clammy cavern were four hundred losers—a mob of miserable humanity. They came from all over and wound up all together. Listen to the account:

> *And everyone who was in distress, and everyone who was in debt, and everyone who was discontented, gathered. . . . There were about four hundred men . . .* (1 Samuel 22:2).

The original Mafia. They all had one thing in common—a bad record. The place smelled like the Rams' locker room and sounded like an Army barracks. You can bet not one of those guys every heard Gothard's principles on handling irritations. They were so tough they'd make Al Capone sleep with a night light. They were gross. Anybody who got near that gang stayed as quiet as a roomful of nuns. They had a quaint name for those who crossed their paths . . . *victims.*

Except for David. That's right. *David.* It became his responsibility to turn that mob into an organized, well-disciplined fighting force . . . mighty men of valor. Talk about a challenge! These weren't the filthy five, nor the nasty nine, nor the dirty dozen. Remember—there were four hundred of these hard luck hooligans. Shortly thereafter, their numbers swelled to six hundred. And David was the den mother for these desperados. He was general, master sergeant, and chaplain all rolled into one. David, "the sweet psalmist of Israel," became David the drill instructor. Needless to say, his battalion of 600 is not to be confused with the 600 who "rode into the valley of death" in Tennyson's *Charge of the Light Brigade*. The only place these guys had ridden was out of town, chased by their creditors . . . which turned David's men into predators.

Did he pull it off? Could a shepherd from Bethlehem assume command of such a nefarious band of ne'er-do-wells? Did he meet the challenge?

INDEED!

In a brief period of time he had the troops in shape—combat ready. Incredible as it seems, he was doing battle against the enemy forces using strategic maneuvers before the year was up. These were the very men who fought loyally by his side and gave him strong support when he became the king of Israel. They were called "the mighty men" and many of their names were listed in the Bible for heroism and dedication.

All of us face a challenge. For some of you, it's a business that has all the earmarks of disaster. For others, it's the challenge of schooling without adequate money, or a houseful of young lives to shape, or a wounded relationship, or a prolonged illness that lingers and hurts. Still others of you find yourself in leadership over a group of people who need constant direction and encouragement . . . and you're tired of the demands. Some of you endure employment in a company that lacks a lot.

Be encouraged! If David could handle that cave full of malcontents . . . you can tighten your belt and take on the challenge in *your* cave. Do you need strength? Peace? Wisdom? Direction? Discipline? Ask for it! God will hear you. He gives special attention to cries when they come out of caves.

Secret Wounds,
Silent Cries

T*ucked away in* a quiet corner of
Scripture is a verse that brims with emotion. Read slowly and thoughtfully these ancient words from the pen
of Job:

> *From the city men groan, and the souls of the wounded cry out*
> . . . (Job 24:12).

Slip into that scene . . . a busy metropolis . . . speed . . . movement . . .
noise. Rows of buildings, acres of apartments, miles of houses, restau-

rants, stores, cars, bikes, kids. All of that is obvious. Any city-dweller could describe the scene, delineate the action.

But there is more. Behind and beneath the loud splash of human activity are invisible aches. Job calls them "groans." In Hebrew the word suggests that this groan comes from one who has been *wounded*. Perhaps that is why Job adds the next line in poetic form, "the souls of the wounded cry out. . . ." In that line, "wounded" comes from a term that means "pierced," *as if stabbed*. Not a physical stabbing—for it is "the soul" that is crying out. What does he mean?

There are those who suffer from the blows of "soul stabbing," wounds which can be far more painful and devastating than "body stabbing." Job has reference to deep lacerations of the heart—invisible, internal injuries no surgeon in the world could detect. The city is full of such hurts. It's a desolate, disturbing scene . . . but painfully true. Wounded, broken, bruised, many a person cries out with groans from the innermost being.

Perhaps that describes *you* today. You may be "groaning" because you've been misunderstood or treated unfairly. The injury is deep because the blow landed from someone you trust and respect . . . someone you are vulnerable to . . . someone you love. It is possible that your pain was inflicted by the stabbing of someone's tongue. They are saying things that are simply untrue—but to step in and set the record straight would seem defensive or inappropriate. Perhaps the comment was made only in passing, but it cut into the tissue, it pierced you deeply. The person who made the remark will never know. But you will . . . as you endure . . . keep quiet . . . and bleed.

> *And many a word, at random spoken,*
> *May soothe or wound a heart that's broken.*
>
> (SIR WALTER SCOTT)

Quite probably others of you are living with scars brought on by past sins or failures. Although you have confessed and forsaken those ugly, bitter days, you can't seem to erase the backwash. Sometimes when you're alone the past slips up from behind like a freak ocean wave and overwhelms you. The scab is jarred loose. The wound stays inflamed and tender and you wonder if it will *ever* go away. Although it is unknown to others, you live in the fear of being found out . . . and rejected.

It was Amy Carmichael who once helped heal a wound within me and turn it into a scar of beauty instead of disgrace. I share with you her words:

NO SCAR?

Hast thou no scar?
NO hidden scar on foot, or side, or hand?
I hear thee sung as mighty in the land,
I hear them hail thy bright ascendant star,
Hast thou no scar?

Hast thou no wound?
Yet I was wounded by the archers, spent,
Leaned Me against a tree to die; and rent
By ravening beasts that compassed Me,
I swooned:
Hast thou no wound?

No wound, no scar?
Yet, as the Master shall the servant be,
And, pierced are the feet that follow Me;
But thine are whole: can he have followed far
Who has no wound nor scar?

Tucked away in a quiet corner of *every* life are wounds and scars. If they were not there, we would need no Physician. Nor would we need one another.

Photograph by Mark Veldheer

After the Avalanche

~

Job *wrote about* wounds. His words were more than patronizing platitudes and armchair proverbs. He'd been there and back again. He could describe intense inner suffering in the first person because of his own sea of pain.

Step into the time tunnel with me and let's travel together back to Uz (not like the Wizard of but like the land of). Wherever it was, Uz had a citizen who had the respect of everyone, since he was blameless, upright,

God-fearing, and clean-living. He had ten children, fields of livestock, an abundance of land, a houseful of servants, and a substantial stack of cash. No one would deny that the man called Job was "the greatest of the men of the East." He had earned that title through years of hard work and honest dealings with others. His very name was a synonym for integrity and godliness.

Then without announcement, adversity thundered upon him like an avalanche of great, jagged rocks. He lost his livestock, crops, land, servants, and—if you can believe it—all ten children. Soon thereafter he lost his health, his last human hope of earning a living. I plead with you to stop reading, set the book in your lap, close your eyes for sixty seconds, and identify with that good man—crushed beneath the weight of adversity.

The book that bears his name records an entry he made into his journal soon after the rocks stopped falling and the dust began to settle. With a quivering hand, the man from Uz wrote:

*Naked I came from my mother's womb, And naked I shall
return there. The LORD gave and the LORD has taken away. Blessed
be the name of the LORD* (Job 1:21).

Following this incredible statement, God adds:

Through all this Job did not sin nor did he blame God (1:22).

Right about now I'm shaking my head. How could anyone handle
such a series of grief-laden ordeals so calmly? Think of the aftermath:
bankruptcy, pain, ten fresh graves . . . the loneliness of those empty
rooms. Yet we read that he worshiped God, he did not sin, nor did he
blame his Maker.

Well, why didn't he? How could he keep from it? How could he ward
off the bitterness or ignore thoughts of suicide? At the risk of oversimpli-
fying the situation, I suggest three basic answers:

First, *Job claimed God's loving sovereignty.* He sincerely believed that the Lord who gave had every right to take away (Job 1:21). Stated in his own words:

Shall we indeed accept good from God and not accept adversity? (Job 2:10).

He looked *up*, claiming his Lord's right to rule over his life. Who is the fool that says God has no right to add sand to our clay or marks to our vessel or fire to His workmanship? Who dares lift his clay fist heavenward and question the Potter's plan? Not Job! To him, God's sovereignty was laced with His love.

Second, *he counted on the promise of resurrection*. Do you remember his immortal words?

. . . I know that my Redeemer lives, And at the last . . . I shall see God (Job 19:25–26).

He looked *ahead*, counting on his Lord's promise to make all things bright and beautiful in the life beyond. He knew that at *that* time, all pain, death, sorrow, tears, and adversity would be removed. Knowing that "hope does not disappoint" (Romans 5:5) he endured today by envisioning tomorrow.

Third, *he confessed his own lack of understanding.* What a relief this brings! Job didn't feel obligated to explain the "whys" of his situation. Listen to his admission of this fact:

> *I know that Thou canst do all things, And that no purpose of Thine can be thwarted. . . . Therefore I have declared that which I did not understand, Things too wonderful [too deep] for me, which I did not know. . . . "I will ask Thee, and do Thou instruct me"* (Job 42:2–4).

Third, he looked *within,* confessing his inability to put it all together. Resting his case with the righteous Judge, Job did not feel compelled to answer all the questions or unravel all the burning riddles. God would judge. The Judge would be right.

Could it be that you are beginning to feel the nick of falling rocks? Maybe the avalanche has already fallen . . . maybe not. Adversity may seem ten thousand miles away . . . as remote as the land of Uz. That's the way Job felt just a few minutes before the landslide.

Review these thoughts as you turn out the lights tonight, my friend, just in case. Consider Job's method for picking up the pieces.

Cloudless days are fine but remember: Some pottery gets pretty fragile sitting in the sun day after day after day.

WORM THEOLOGY

Ever get a song on your mind? Sure, it happens to everyone. It can drive you crazy . . . like a silly commercial jingle. The Madison Avenue guy makes them that way—so they'll stick like cockleburs to a spaniel's ear. Sometimes, however, the melody on the brain is a welcome one. Like a solid, old hymn that keeps us company during a lonely afternoon.

It happened to me last week. Isaac Watts struck again. One of his best (he wrote over six hundred!) lingered in my head for more than an hour before I actually formed the words with my mouth. Suddenly, I found myself listening to what Watts wrote over two centuries ago:

Alas! and did my Savior bleed?
And did my Sovereign die?
Would He devote that sacred head
For such a worm as I?

I frowned as that last line faded away. A worm? Does God see people as worms? When Christ died did He "devote that sacred head" for *worms?* Now, obviously, Watts wanted to portray a vivid illustration of sinful mankind—lost, undeserving, spiritually worthless, wicked within. Dipping his brush in Job 25 and Isaiah 41, the hymnist painted such a picture, using the very term Scripture uses—worm. He was biblical and therefore justified in his choice of terms for the text. Frankly, we were worm-like when our righteous God found us—lowly, wandering, dirty, unattractive, grubby creatures.

But that doesn't mean we work hard at making ourselves into worms now. *A child of God is not a worm.* If God had wanted you to be a worm, He could have very easily made you one! He's very good at worms, you know. There's an infinite variety of the wriggly creatures. When Watts wrote of worms, he was merely using a word picture. Many others, however, have framed it as a model to follow, calling it humility. This "worm theology" creates enormous problems.

It wears many faces—all sad. It crawls out from between the mattress and the springs in the morning, telling itself, "I'm nothing. I'm a worm. Woe, woe. I can't do anything and even if I appear to be doing something, it's not really me. Woe! I must annihilate self respect . . . crucify all motivation and ambition. If any good accidentally leaks out, I must quickly hide it or categorically deny I had anything to do with it. How could I accomplish anything of value? I mean, who am I? I'm a worm. Good for nothing except crawling very slowly, drowning in mud puddles, or getting stepped on. Woe, woe, woe."

There's one main problem with this sort of thinking—it's *phony*. No matter how diligently we labor to appear genuinely humble, it amounts to nothing more than trying to look good in another way. Self-made worms carry around little signs you have to squint at to read:

I bet I'm twice as humble as you.

And therein lies the ugly sin: PRIDE.

Heretical though it may sound, no one who actually hates himself can adequately share the love of Christ. Our Lord taught that we were to love our neighbors *as we love ourselves*. Think that over. If we don't properly love ourselves, where does that leave our neighbors? I have yet to witness an effective, happy, fulfilled Christian whose image of himself was poor . . . who *really* believed he was a worm.

Have you taken time this week to consider before your Lord and His Word who you really are? It's impossible to imagine that one who is adopted into God's family, accepted in the Beloved, a recipient of the riches of Christ, called to be His ambassador, and the object of infinite grace, mercy, love, and peace, ought to slither around like a nightcrawler. If you ask me, *that's* heresy!

Sinful? Oh yes. Undeserving? Absolutely. Imperfect? Who isn't! Selfish? Indeed! Wrong? More often than not.

But a *worm?* Useless? Unimportant? Spineless? Meaningless? No, not that. God declared us righteous. He lifted us out of the miry clay and set us upon a rock. He invites us to approach Him with boldness. And He means it!

No condemnation now I dread;
Jesus, and all in Him is mine!
Alive in Him, my living Head,
And clothed in righteousness Divine,
Bold, I approach the eternal throne,
And claim the crown, through Christ my own.

Now *there's* a song to get stuck in your mind.

The Road Beyond

*"It is His love that arranges our tomorrows . . .
and we may be certain that whatever it brings,
His love sent it our way."*

TOMORROW

I *was driving up* to Forest Home with easy listening music crooning through the speaker. A quiet drive on a mellow Sunday afternoon. Then I saw something up ahead. Before I realized what it was, it flashed in my mind as something terribly wrong—out of place—distorted.

An overturned car—I could see it now. An ambulance screamed somewhere back. I felt like someone had pushed a fist into my stomach. Directing traffic around the accident, a highway patrolman briskly motioned on the crawling line of cars. I got too close of a look at the

Photograph ©1991 Gary Irving

vehicle resting on its crumpled top. The scene hangs in my mind . . . the bystanders staring in open-mouthed disbelief . . . two men dragging limp bodies out of the wreckage onto the pavement. All of the passengers were either dead or terribly mutilated.

Such a warm, peaceful Sunday. The day was bright and filled with leisure hours. But for three people, that moment the world flipped—violently, crazily, fatally—upside down. What appeared to be another day of "fun-'n-games" became a day of infamous calamity. Naturally, I wondered if those victims knew our Lord—if they could smile at eternity. My pulse shot up so that I had to grip the wheel with both hands. Under my breath, I mumbled Proverbs 27:1:

> *Do not boast about tomorrow, for you do not know what a day may bring forth.*

James 4:13–14 was certainly written with that particular proverb in mind. I said it out loud—several times—as the traffic resumed speed and scattered heedless across the afternoon.

Come now, you who say, "Today or tomorrow, we shall go to such and such a city, and spend a year there and engage in business and make a profit." Yet you do not know what your life will be like tomorrow. You are just a vapor that appears for a little while and then vanishes away.

Sit down for a moment, please. Find a quiet spot in your dwelling . . . just for sixty seconds. Think—just think about the two statements: ". . . you do not know what your life will be like tomorrow . . ." and ". . . you do not know what a day may bring forth."

Man's knowledge seems impressive—awesome. We can split atoms, we can build skyscrapers, transplant kidneys, program computers, explore and explain outer space, and even unknot the problems of ecology. But when it comes to *tomorrow,* our knowledge plunges to zero. Whoever you are. You may be a Ph.D. from Yale, you may be a genius in your field with an IQ above 170, marvelously gifted and totally capable in any number of advanced, technological specialties—but you simply *do not know* what tomorrow will bring. Scientists may project, program, predict, deduct, deduce, and compute diagrams about the future. They're still only guessing. In algebraic terms, tomorrow remains factor X—a mystery. It cannot be explained. It defies all attempts to be exposed. It lies hidden in the depths of God's unfathomable, intricately interwoven plan. He has not been pleased to unveil it until this old earth spins sufficiently to see the dawn. And then . . . only one moment at a time.

Tomorrow. It may bring sickness, sorrow, or tragedy. It may announce an answer to your waiting prayer. It may introduce you to prosperity, the beginning of a friendship, a choice opportunity for sharing your Lord . . . or just another twenty-four hours of waiting, trusting, and claiming His presence. It may not even come. God may choose this very day to intervene and take you Home—either by death or by rapture. We can speculate, we can dread, we can dream—but we do not know.

This sort of thinking leads to an inevitable question: Are you ready? "Ready for what?" you may ask. "Ready for *anything*" is my answer. Is your trust, your attitude of dependence, sufficiently stable to sustain you *regardless?* Remember Job's avalanche? Should your Lord be pleased to turn you into a Job, would He still be your Treasure and your Triumph? Don't let the answer slip off your tongue too easily. Think about the implications of that question to your own life, health, job, and family. Should your Lord make you an Enoch, would you be reluctant to make that eternal journey?

Thank the Lord, it is His *love* that arranges our tomorrows . . . and we may be certain that whatever it brings, His love sent it our way. That is why I smile every time I read Romans 11:33. Let it bring a smile into your world.

> *Oh, what a wonderful God we have! How great are his wisdom and knowledge and riches! How impossible it is for us to under-stand his decisions and his methods!* (TLB).

CLEAR VIEW FROM MT. PERSPECTIVE

The coed had two problems common to many students: low grades and no money. She was forced to communicate both to her parents, whom she knew would have trouble understanding. After considerable thought she used a creative approach to soften the blows of reality. She wrote the following letter:

Dear Mom and Dad,
Just thought I'd drop you a note to clue you in on my plans. I've

Photograph by Mark Veldheer

fallen in love with a guy named Jim. He quit high school after grade eleven to get married. About a year ago he got a divorce.

We've been going steady for two months and plan to get married in the fall. Until then, I've decided to move into his apartment (I think I might be pregnant).

At any rate, I dropped out of school last week, although I'd like to finish college some time in the future.

On the next page she continued:

Mom and Dad, I just want you to know that everything I've written so far in this letter is false. NONE of it is true.

But Mom and Dad, it IS true that I got a C- in French and flunked Math. . . . It IS true that I'm going to need some more money for my tuition payments.

Pretty sharp coed! Even bad news can sound like good news if it is seen from a certain vantage point. So much in life depends on where you're coming from as you face your circumstances. The secret, of course, is perspective.

And what *is* perspective? Obviously, it's related to the way we view something. The term literally suggests "looking through . . . seeing clearly." One who views life through perspective lenses has the capacity to see things in their true relations or relative importance. He scopes in on the big picture. He distinguishes the incidental from the essential . . . the temporary from the eternal . . . the partial from the whole . . . the trees from the forest.

For the next few minutes, snap a telescopic lens on your perspective and pull yourself up close. Close enough to see the *real* you. Study what you see. Like a physician giving you a physical. Like an artist painting your portrait. Like a biographer writing your story. From the reflection in your mental mirror, pay close attention to your life. Try your best to examine the inner "you" on the basis of *time*.

Lift yourself above the smothering details of today's tangled thicket and breathe the crisp, fresh air that surrounds the clear view high up on Mt. Perspective. Seems to me the only way to carry out this project is to look in two directions . . . back, then ahead. In many ways what we see in our past and visualize in our future determines how we view ourselves today . . . right now . . . that depth-yielding third dimension we call "the present."

As we look *back,* one overriding thought eclipses all others. It's not very new, nor very profound, but few would debate its truth: LIFE IS SHORT. That's not only a valid observation from experience, it's a constant beacon reflecting from the pages of the Bible. Psalm 90 flashes the truth again and again. Listen to some of the analogies employed by the composer.

Life is short . . . . . . *like yesterday when it passes by (v. 4a) . . . as a watch in the night (v. 4b) . . . like grass . . . it sprouts . . . and withers (vv. 5–6) . . . like a sigh (v. 9) . . . soon it is gone (v. 10)*

Wistful scenes looking back from Mt. Perspective. Standing on that silent summit brings a subtle, perhaps painful reminder that we aren't getting any younger. Life, indeed, is short.

Shifting our position and looking *ahead* at the opposite horizon, we discern another singular message. Again, the words are neither unique nor scholarly—but they echo back repeatedly: LIFE IS UNCERTAIN. A single adjective could precede most every event in our future: unexpected. Unexpected . . . surgery, transfer, change, accomplishment, loss, benefit, sickness, promotion, demotion, gift, death. Life, indeed, is uncertain.

James (4:13–15) verifies both these thoughts. He says that our lives are merely vapors that appear then vanish (life is short). He also says that we do not know what our lives will be like tomorrow (life is uncertain). Professor Time, that venerable pedagogue, teaches us both lessons well. We are wise to remember them.

Well then, what about today? Since life is brief and so unsure, how should we view our present? Most philosophers offer advice that is dangerously near despair, or at best, discontentment. Spend enough time soaking up their stuff and you'll become as grim-faced as a New York pickpocket—and just as much in demand. John Keats was right—*Philosophy will clip an angel's wings.*

I suggest there are three words which adequately and accurately describe the present. They do not contradict either of the lessons we've learned on the peaks of Mt. Perspective. Nor do they require rose-colored glasses. Neither do they agree with the futile meanderings of modern philosophy. Looking to the present, we discover: LIFE IS CHALLENGING. Because it is short, every moment wells up challenging possibilities. Because it is uncertain, it's filled with challenging adjustments. Could this be what Jesus referred to when He promised an *abundant* life? Abundant with challenges, brimming with possibilities, spilling over with opportunities to adapt, shift, alter, and change. This is the perspective that keeps people young. It is also the path that leads to optimism and motivation.

Every new dawn, before you awaken, life makes a delivery to your front door, rings the doorbell, and runs. Each package is cleverly wrapped. Put together they comprise a series of challenging opportunities brilliantly disguised as unsolvable problems. They are wrapped in paper with big print. One package reads: "Watch out—better worry about this!" Another: "Danger—this will bring fear!" And another: "Impossible—you'll never handle this one!"

When you hear the ring in the morning, try something new.

Have Jesus Christ answer the door for you.

THE CASE
AGAINST VANILLA

I *cannot imagine* anything more boring and less desirable than being poured into the mold of predictability as I grow older. Few things interest me less than the routine, the norm, the expected, the status quo. Call it the rebel in me, but I simply cannot bear plain vanilla when life offers so many other colorful and stimulating flavors. A fresh run at life by an untried route will get my vote every time—in spite of the risk. Stay open-minded for a moment and I'll try to show you why.

John Gardner once pointed out that by their mid-thirties, most people have stopped acquiring new skills and new attitudes in any aspect of their lives. Does that jolt you? Stop and think, you who are over thirty. How long has it been since *you* acquired a new skill? How many brand-new attitudes have you adopted—personal, political, social, spiritual, financial—since you turned thirty?

Let's probe a little deeper. Do you drive to work the same way every morning? Are you compelled to approach a problem the identical way every time? Does a maverick (even *wild*) idea challenge you or cause you to retreat into the security of your shell? Have you lost that enthusiastic zest for discovery and adventure? Say, you're older than you thought. You're older than you ought! God has arranged an abundant life for you, but it's slipping past. You're fast becoming addicted to the narcotic of predictability . . . and the longer you persist, the greater will be the pain of withdrawal.

Living and learning are linked; so are existing and expiring. Each day delivers a totally new set of circumstances and experiences. The same hours and minutes which capture the wonder of a child may deepen the rut of an adult. Ever watched a preschooler's approach to life? His constant curiosity and probing inquisitiveness make every day completely fresh and exciting. To him, learning is natural; to the adult, it's a nuisance.

"Well," you rationalize, "I'm just too set. That's the way I am . . . you can't change me." *Who* can't change you? *God?* Like Israel of old, this sort of thinking puts limits on the Lord, discounting His power and denying His presence. Settling down to the hum-drum, bland diet of tasteless existence is a sure invitation for slackness and indolence to invade and plague your dwelling.

"So, how do I break out?" you ask. "I guess I could row to Hawaii in a four-foot dinghy or schedule a February vacation in Iceland . . . maybe the family could tackle Everest this summer. . . ."

Unnecessary! Life abounds with everyday problems needing transformation into creative projects. Try taking life by the throat and achieve mastery over a few things that have haunted and harassed you long enough. Or—how about a course at a nearby school this fall . . . or a serious study of some subject all on your own. Why not broaden yourself in some *new* way to the greater glory of God?

Remember our old friend, Caleb? He was eighty-five and still growing when he gripped an uncertain future and put the torch to the bridges behind him. At a time when the ease and comfort of retirement seemed predictable, he fearlessly faced the invincible giants of the mountain. Read Joshua 14 again. There was no dust on that fella. Every new sunrise introduced another reminder that his body and a rocking chair weren't made for each other. While his peers were yawning, Caleb was yearning.

Every one of us was poured into a mold . . . but some are "moldier" than others. If you are determined and work quickly, you can keep the concrete of predictability from setting rock-hard up to your ears. Then again, if the risks and potential dangers of sailing your ship in the vast oceans of uncertainty make you seasick, you'd better anchor yourself near the shallow shore of security. Concrete sinks fast, you know.

Photograph by Mark Veldheer

GOD'S CONTROL

The bitter news of Dawson Trotman's drowning swept like cold wind across Schroon Lake to the shoreline. Eyewitnesses tell of the profound anxiety, the tears, the helpless disbelief in the faces of those who now looked out across the deep blue water. Everyone's face except one—Lila Trotman, Dawson's widow. As she suddenly walked upon the scene a close friend shouted, "Oh, Lila . . . he's gone. Dawson's gone!" To that she replied in calm assurance the words of Psalm 115:3:

But our God is in the heavens; He does whatever He pleases.

All of the anguish, the sudden loneliness that normally consumes and cripples those who survive did not invade that woman's heart. Instead, she leaned hard upon her sovereign Lord, who had once again done what He pleased.

As you read these words . . . does that seem strange to you? Does it seem unusual to refer to a tragic death as being God's pleasure? Honestly now, do you think God's control over us is total . . . or partial? Let's allow His Word to speak on this deep subject:

Thou hast enclosed me behind and before, And laid Thy hand upon me. Thine eyes have seen my unformed substance; And in Thy book they were all written, The days that were ordained for me, When as yet there was not one of them (Psalm 139:5,16).

Woe to the one who quarrels with his Maker— An earthenware vessel among the vessels of earth! Will the clay say to the potter, "What are you doing?" (Isaiah 45:9).

. . . I am God, and there is no other; I am God, and there is no one like Me . . . Saying, "My purpose will be established, And I

will accomplish all My good pleasure" (Isaiah 46:9–10).

He does according to His will in the host of heaven And among the inhabitants of earth; And no one can ward off His hand Or say to Him, "What hast Thou done?" (Daniel 4:35).

There are more. Patiently, repeatedly, in a dozen different ways the Word makes the point. Accept it or not, God's calling the shots. He's running the show. Either He's in *full* control or He's off His throne. It's as foolish to say He is "almost sovereign" as it would be to say I'm "almost married" or Kennedy was "almost president" or the surgeon's gloves are "almost sterile."

If you're trying to grasp all the ramifications of this great truth . . . don't. You can't anyway. Feverishly toiling to unravel all the knots can turn you into a fanatical freak . . . it will push you to the edge of your mental capacity . . . it will result in endless hours of theological hairsplitting. The finite can *never* plumb the depths of the infinite . . . so don't waste your time trying. There's no way you'll ever fully reconcile God's control over all events and man's responsibility . . . the justice of God and the heartaches of man . . . our Lord's supreme control and this earth's inequities, tragedies, and injustices. No way.

It was a glorious day when I was liberated from the concentration camp of fear . . . the fear of saying, "I don't understand the reasons why, but I accept God's hand in what has happened." It was a *greater* day when I realized that nobody expected me to have all the answers . . . least of all God! If I could figure it all out, I'd qualify as His adviser, and Scripture makes it clear He doesn't need my puny counsel. He wants my unreserved love, my unqualified devotion, my undaunted trust—not my unenlightened analysis of His ways.

One of the marks of spiritual maturity is the quiet confidence that God is in control . . . without the need to understand why He does what He does. Lila Trotman bore such a mark as she faced the ways of God that were "unsearchable . . . and unfathomable."

What marks *your* life?

GOING ... NOT KNOWING

The statement recurs through Scripture like a repeating telegraph signal on a high frequency radio band. Sometimes faint, barely discernible—sometimes strong, clear. Over and over. Paul made the statement as he was saying goodbye to a group of friends standing with him on an Asian beach. Several of the men wept freely, realizing they would never see the missionary again. The aging apostle looked from man to man, holding each one's eyes for a brief moment. Then, looking out to sea

with his weathered hand pointing south to the stormy skies above the Mediterranean, he voiced these words:

And now, in obedience to the Holy Spirit I am going to Jerusalem, not knowing what will happen to me there (Acts 20:22, Good News Bible).

What an honest admission!

. . . I am going . . . not knowing what will happen . . .

That's what this thing called the Christian life is all about, isn't it? Going . . . yet not knowing. As followers of our Lord we believe He leads us in a certain direction . . . or in pursuit of a precise goal. That leading is unmistakably clear. Not necessarily logical nor explainable, but clear. At least *to us*. So—out of sheer obedience—we go. We pack our bags, pull up stakes, bid our friends farewell, and strike out. We face a future as uncertain as our leading is sure. How strange . . . yet how typical!

There isn't a Christian reading my words who hasn't walked that path. And struggled with ways to convince others it was right. And endured the frowns and well-meaning counsel of those who tried to point out why the idea was a fluke . . . even downright foolish.

For sure Abraham faced it when he wrenched up roots from his hometown soil and struck out for—let's see, where *was* he going? He didn't know! There he was, almost seventy-five years old, loading up a camel caravan with his wife and family bound for . . . *somewhere*. Hebrews 11:8 puts it straight:

> *By faith Abraham, when he was called, obeyed by going out . . . not knowing where he was going.*

"Abraham, what are you doing?" asked a neighbor.

"I'm packing."

"Packing?"

"That's right. We're moving."

"Why? Why in the world would you want to leave Ur?"

"God has made it clear that I should go."

"God, huh? You've been talking to Him again?"

"Right. He told me to leave. I *must* go."

"Well, where are you going?"

"I don't know. He didn't tell me that."

"Wait a minute. Let me get this straight. You *know* you oughta go, but you don't know much beyond that, huh?"

"That says it pretty well."

"Wow . . . that's all I can say . . . wow. God sure gets blamed for a lot of stuff He doesn't have anything to do with. You know, man, some of us have been a little bit worried about the way you've been acting lately. Up to now, it's just been a little strange . . . but this, Abraham . . . this takes you off the end of the pier. It's like everyone's saying—you really *are* off the deep end!"

And so it goes. Who hasn't stepped off the end of the dock to stride on faith footing? It is no easy thing to leave a sure thing, walk away from an ace in the hole, and start down a long, dark tunnel with no end in sight. Absolutely frightening . . . yet filled with unimaginable excitement. Going . . . yet not knowing. Obeying . . . yet not understanding. Beginning a journey that is unpredictable, risky, untried, and appearing virtually insane—yet prompted by none other than the Lord Himself.

Like the competent Christian businessman I spoke to who left a secure $100,000-a-year position to enter a whole new career without training or expertise in the field. After he learns the ropes he may (repeat *may*) gross $20,000, if things fall together. "Why?" I asked. With incredible assurance he answered, "One word—*God*." I've seldom seen a person more confident, more fulfilled.

Are you on the verge of such a decision? Is the Lord loosening your tent pegs today, suggesting it's time for you to take a drastic leap of faith? Are you counting on Him to direct your steps through a future that offers no tangible map? Great! But before you jump, be sure of four things:

Be sure it's the Lord who is speaking.

Be sure the decision doesn't contradict Scripture.

Be sure your motive is unselfish and pure.

Be sure the "leap" won't injure others or your testimony.

Sometimes it helps to remember what God calls us during our short stint on Planet Earth: strangers and pilgrims. People on the move, living in tents, free and unencumbered, loose and available, ready to roll, willing to break the mold—whenever and wherever He leads. Regardless.

THE LONELY TRAIL
OF THE GIMPER

You *won't find* one in the *National Wildlife Federation's Manual of Rare Species.* But rare it is.

Like the bald eagle, the prairie bison, and the whooping crane, gimpers are seldom seen on our landscapes. Occasional sightings, however, have reportedly occurred on college campuses, athletic teams, in business offices, rest homes, and among groups of salesmen. Look closely, and you may even run across a few in some churches. In fact, though their appearances are seldom, gimpers form the backbone of whatever they're a part of. One of the reasons they're so hard to spot is that they never run in packs. They're loners.

Okay, so what is a gimper, anyway? Plug these clues into your computer program and see if you can come up with a revealing readout:

In the 1976 Summer Olympics, Bruce Jenner was a *gimper*.

In the six-day war, so was Moshe Dayan.

As a football strategist, Vince Lombardi qualified.

A *gimper* of motherhood was Susanna Wesley.

Donald Barnhouse was a *gimper* preacher.

As a creative thinker, da Vinci belonged to the club.

A *gimper* president was Abe Lincoln.

Thomas Edison was a *gimper* inventor.

Jim Elliot and Nate Saint were *gimper* missionaries.

And there are others much less famous but equally impressive. You might even have one in your own family and not know it. Jesse's youngest son David was one—but it caught his dad unaware.

Still can't figure it out? Maybe you'd better huddle with Webster for a minute or two. No—scratch that. Don't bother. It isn't there. A few dictionaries include *gimp*, however, which means "spirit, vim, vigor, ambition."

My own first encounter with *gimper* was many years ago in the writing of Dr. M. R. DeHaan. The gravel-voiced, great-hearted teacher of the Radio Bible Class mentioned a gimper as "one who aspires to excel, to be different." A gimper is committed to the core—thoroughly and unequivocally. His roots of dedication result in the rich fruit of determination, excellence, and achievement. Setting their sights high, gimpers drive toward the goal, absorbed in the passion of quality—accomplished at almost any cost.

Now you're getting the picture. Right? Your mind is probably leaping to that graphic Old Testament gimper . . . Jabez. First Chronicles 4:9–10 records the compelling prayer of a unique man who refused to be satisfied with an ordinary, brand-x, milktoast life. You'd never catch Jabez praying, "Dear God, help me to balance my status with my quo. Keep me satisfied in Dullsville, Israel." Not a chance. He pleaded with the Lord to bless him *indeed* . . . to *enlarge* the borders of his perspective . . . and God did just that! It pleased Jehovah to break the predictable mold and launch into society a visionary missile named Jabez.

Did the Lord Jesus make reference to gimpers? No doubt about it. In no uncertain terms He implied how important these rare individuals were to Him when He delivered His immortal mountain message. People ask you to go a mile? Be a gimper, go *two*. Others love their friends and hate their enemies? Gimpers love their enemies and pray for their persecutors! And catch this:

> . . . *if you greet your brothers only, what do you do more than others?* (Matthew 5:47).

Read that one again. That's what gimpers ask. It's the first question in the gimper's manual: "What do you do *more* than others?"

Dotted through the New Testament are references to *abounding* and *excelling*. Each time I run my finger across one of those power lines, I'm challenged to be a gimper.

We are to be gimper givers (2 Corinthians 8:7).

Our walk is to be a gimper walk (1 Thessalonians 4:1).

We should have a gimper love for others (1 Thessalonians 4:10).

The average Christian rejoices; gimper Christians rejoice *always*. Most of us pray; gimpers pray *without ceasing*. It's common to give thanks; gimpers give thanks *in everything*. The basic believer wants to refrain from evil; gimper believers abstain form *every form* of evil (1 Thessalonians 5:16–22).

At age twenty-five, Amaziah was crowned king over Jerusalem. At age fifty-four, he died. For twenty-nine years he did right, according to 2 Chronicles 25:1–2. That's correct—he did right. Stuck to the rules, made all the necessary appearances, smiled when he was supposed to, and looked dignified when protocol required it. As a king, he did right. But God candidly adds, ". . . yet not with a whole heart." He wasn't *whole-heartedly,* hook-line-and-sinker sold out to righteousness. He got by. He yawned his way through almost three decades of history. He punched in at eight o'clock sharp, took a half hour for lunch, and punched out at five. For twenty-nine years. Like the muddy Mississippi, he just kept rolling along.

How different Paul was! In his own words, "steadfast, immovable, always abounding. . . ." Unlike the river, he didn't just roll—he *ricocheted!* He didn't just live life—he *attacked* it. Paul made slothful saints about as comfortable as sleeping on a coat hanger. Nobody every wanted to "gimp" as much as he.

Unless it be thee. Or me.

Wanna race?

THE ROAD AND THE BRIDGE

For more than forty years I've been running. The road behind me rambles over rugged and risky terrain. The road beneath offers more of the same. Every road I've taken, every race I've entered has required a second wind—that afterburner burst of new hope and fresh determination.

What is it that breathes new energy into our weariness, new vision into our discouragement? For me it's the feel of a bridge under my stumbling feet. A strong and stable arch to get me through the wastelands and over the washed out places . . . the low tides, the storms, the winds, the wounds, the aftermath of avalanches.

I'm sure the road beyond won't be much different. I'll still need fresh hope. I'll still need a bridge to span the spots I cannot handle alone. The bridge is neither a philosophy nor a dream. The bridge is a Person. Christ Jesus the Lord. The only One who can stabilize me when everyone and everything fades, fails, and falls.

Do you know Him . . . I mean *really know Him?* If so, RUN. Fix your eyes on Him and refuse to give up or turn back. If not, STOP. Give Him your struggles and receive Him by faith.

He has all the strength you need to keep you on your road.

Put both feet on the Bridge. Meet the real Author of the second wind.